Let's Meet
Sojourner Truth

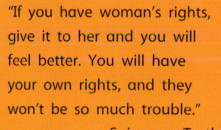

"If you have woman's rights, give it to her and you will feel better. You will have your own rights, and they won't be so much trouble."
–Sojourner Truth

Lisa Trumbauer

CHELSEA CLUBHOUSE
An Imprint of Chelsea House Publishers
A Haights Cross Communications Company
Philadelphia

Chelsea Clubhouse books are published by Chelsea House Publishers,
a subsidiary of Haights Cross Communications.

A Haights Cross Communications Company

The Chelsea House World Wide Web address is www.chelseahouse.com

Printed and bound in the United States of America.
9 8 7 6 5 4 3 2 1

Library of Congress Cataloging-in-Publication Data
Trumbauer, Lisa, 1963–
    Let's meet Sojourner Truth / Lisa Trumbauer.
        p. cm. — (Let's meet biographies)
Summary: Simple text and photographs introduce the life of Sojourner Truth, describing her childhood, life as a slave, freedom, and work as an activist for civil rights and women's right to vote.
Includes bibliographical references and index.
ISBN 0-7910-7323-8
1. Truth, Sojourner, d. 1883—Juvenile literature. 2. African American abolitionists—Biography—Juvenile literature. 3. African American women—Biography—Juvenile literature. 4. Abolitionists—United States—Biography—Juvenile literature. 5. Social reformers—United States—Biography—Juvenile literature. [1. Truth, Sojourner, d. 1883. 2. Abolitionists. 3. Reformers. 4. African Americans—Biography. 5. Women—Biography.] I. Title. II. Series.
E185.97.T8T78 2004
305.5'67'092—dc21   2003004746

Editorial Credits

Lois Wallentine, editor; Takeshi Takahashi, designer; Mary Englar, photo researcher; Keith Trego, layout

Editor's note:

Books about Sojourner Truth vary in their dates and descriptions of events, spellings of names, and wording of quotations. Information in this book draws from the following well-researched biographies: Carleton Mabee, *Sojourner Truth: Slave, Prophet, Legend* (New York: New York University Press, 1993) and Nell Irvin Painter, *Sojourner Truth: A Life, A Symbol* (New York: W.W. Norton & Company, 1996).

Content Reviewer

Mary G. Butler, Director, Research Center, Heritage Battle Creek, Battle Creek, Mich.

Photo Credits

Burton Historical Collection, Detroit Public Library: cover, 21; ©Hulton Archive/by Getty Images Inc.: title page, 9, 10, 20; Senate House State Historic Site, New York State Office of Parks, Recreation and Historic Preservation: 4, 11; ©CORBIS: 5, 6, 26; State Archives of Michigan: 7, 15, 23; The New York Public Library, Picture Collection: 8; Schomburg Center for Research in Black Culture, New York Public Library, Astor, Lenox and Tilden Foundations: 17; ©Bettmann/CORBIS: 12, 13, 14, 16, 24, 29; National Archives: 22; National Portrait Gallery, Smithsonian Institution/Art Resource: 25; Battle Creek Area Chamber of Commerce: 27.

Table of Contents

A Slave Named Isabella   4

Freedom   8

A New Name   14

Speaking the Truth   18

Helping Freed Slaves   22

Important Dates in Sojourner's Life   28
More about the Struggle for Rights   29
Glossary   30
To Learn More   31
Index   32

A Slave Named Isabella

As a child, Sojourner Truth's name was Isabella. Because she was a **slave**, no one wrote down the date of her birth. It is believed to be in 1797.

Isabella's parents were James and Elizabeth. Isabella was close to her younger brother, Peter. Her older brothers and sisters had been sold to other slave owners.

Isabella lived on farms near Rondout Creek, which is shown in this painting.

At a slave auction, people bid on the slaves they wanted to buy. Isabella's new owner bid $100 for her and some sheep.

The Hardenberghs, a **Dutch** family, owned Isabella's family. The Hardenbergh farm was near the town of Hurley, New York.

When Isabella was 11 years old, her master died. She was sold to a new owner at an **auction**. Isabella was forced to leave her family and the only home she knew.

Many slaves prayed to be freed from cruel masters. While living with the Neely family, Isabella asked God to help her get to "a new and better place."

The Neely family bought Isabella. They spoke English. Isabella spoke only Dutch, like the Hardenberghs. She couldn't understand her new owners' orders. Sometimes they beat Isabella when she made mistakes.

After about a year, Isabella was sold again to Martinus Schryver. He was a farmer, fisherman, and innkeeper. He treated Isabella a little better.

In 1810, 13-year-old Isabella was sold a third time. John Dumont bought her to work on his family's farm near New Paltz, New York. Isabella would be the Dumonts' slave for 16 years.

Isabella's Family

When Isabella was about 16 years old, her owner made her marry a slave named Thomas. Isabella had four children. Their names were Diana, Peter, Elizabeth, and Sophia. Isabella may have had another child who died while quite young.

This photograph shows Isabella's daughter Diana in her later years.

7

Freedom

In 1817, a new law passed. It said that on July 4, 1827, most adult slaves in the state would receive their freedom. Dumont said Isabella could be free a year early if she worked very hard. Isabella worked as hard as she could. But in the summer of 1826, her owner said he wouldn't free her.

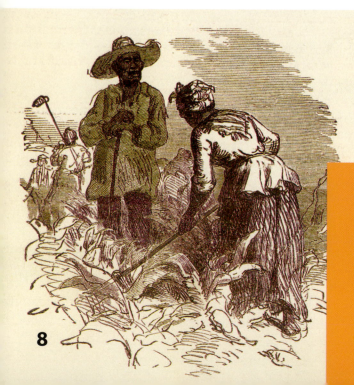

Dumont bragged that Isabella worked as hard as his best men in the fields all day and still did housework at night. But he didn't keep his promise to free her.

Isabella was 29 years old when she became free.

That fall, Isabella decided to free herself. Before dawn one morning, she took her baby, Sophia, and left. She walked several miles to the Van Wagenens' house. These neighbors thought slavery was wrong and agreed to help her.

John Dumont came looking for Isabella. The Van Wagenens paid him $20 for Isabella and $5 for her daughter. Then they said Isabella and Sophia were free.

After Isabella left, Dumont decided to sell her 6-year-old son, Peter, to the Gedney family. Then Solomon Gedney sold Peter to a farmer in Alabama. This sale was against a state law. The law said that a slave in New York could not be sold to a person in another state.

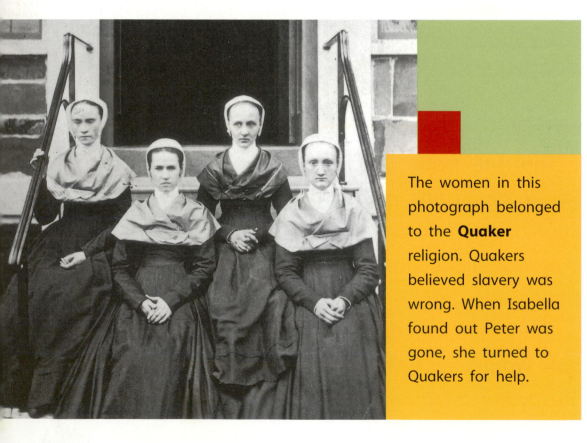

The women in this photograph belonged to the **Quaker** religion. Quakers believed slavery was wrong. When Isabella found out Peter was gone, she turned to Quakers for help.

Isabella's case against Solomon Gedney was heard at this courthouse in Kingston, New York.

Isabella wanted to bring Peter back. In 1827, a group of Quakers helped her press charges against Solomon Gedney. After nearly a year, Gedney brought Peter to the courthouse. A judge listened to the case. No one thought Isabella would win against a white man, but she did. The judge freed Peter to live with his mother.

Many free black women worked as housekeepers for wealthy families. Isabella worked for several families during the 14 years she lived in New York City.

In 1829, Isabella decided to move to New York City with Peter. She wanted Peter to go to school. She planned to find work as a housekeeper. But it would be hard for her to work while taking care of her baby. So Sophia went to live with Isabella's other daughters. They were still slaves on the Dumont farm.

In New York City, Peter skipped school and got into trouble. Finally he took a job on a whaling ship that set sail in 1839. He wrote letters to his mother, but she did not know how to read. Isabella's friends read Peter's letters to her. The last letter arrived in 1841. Isabella never heard from her son again.

Peter took a job on a whaling ship called *Zone*, which may have looked like these ships. Whaling ships sailed long distances while hunting whales for their oil.

13

A New Name

Isabella was unhappy in New York City. She said, "The rich rob the poor, and the poor rob one another."

Isabella had a strong faith in God. She believed God helped her leave the Dumonts and helped her free her son. Now she believed God wanted her to travel and tell her story to others.

Five Points was a dangerous area in New York City. For a time, Isabella joined a group that preached to people in this area about having faith in God.

On June 1, 1843, Isabella changed her name to Sojourner. *Sojourn* means to stay only a short time. Sojourner planned to stay in places long enough to tell others of "the hope that was in her." Then she would move on. Later, she said her last name was Truth, "because I was to declare the truth to the people."

Isabella, now called Sojourner, would spend the next 40 years of her life as a public speaker. This poster was used to announce her lectures, or speeches.

Sojourner preached at many outdoor gatherings like the one shown in this painting. In the 1800s, religious groups would hold camp meetings to listen to speakers and pray together.

Sojourner packed some clothes and a small basket of food. She put 25 cents in her pocket. Then she took a **ferry** to Long Island, New York, and started walking. She walked across the island and then went to Connecticut. She stopped to tell her story wherever she found people gathered for **religious** meetings.

Sojourner became a popular speaker. She was nearly 6 feet (1.8 meters) tall and had a powerful voice. She told stories about her life as a slave and shared her thoughts on faith in God. One listener wrote that "God helps her to pry where but few can."

Sojourner was a lively speaker at meetings. She also was known for her beautiful singing.

Speaking the Truth

NARRATIVE

OF

SOJOURNER TRUTH,

A

NORTHERN SLAVE,

EMANCIPATED FROM BODILY SERVITUDE BY THE STATE OF
NEW YORK, IN 1828.

WITH A PORTRAIT.

'SWEET is the virgin honey, though the wild bee store it in a reed;
And bright the jewelled band that circleth an Ethiop's arm;
Pure are the grains of gold in the turbid stream of the Ganges;
And fair the living flowers that spring from the dull cold sod.
Wherefore, thou gentle student, bow'd thine ear to my speech,
For I also am as thou art; our hearts can commune together:
To meanest matters will I stoop, for mean is the lot of mortal;
I will rise to noblest themes, for the soul hath a heritage of glory.'

BOSTON:
PRINTED FOR THE AUTHOR.
1850.

Sojourner met Olive Gilbert at the Northampton Association. In 1850, Gilbert wrote down Sojourner's life story for the book *The Narrative of Sojourner Truth*. Sojourner earned money by selling this book wherever she spoke.

From 1844 to 1846, Sojourner lived with a group called the Northampton Association. Members lived and worked together. They shared ideas on many topics.

Several members were **abolitionists**. They believed slavery was wrong. They organized **debates** on how best to end slavery. In about 1850, Sojourner started telling her story at abolition meetings.

At meetings, Sojourner also sold her picture, which she called her "shadow," to earn money to support herself.

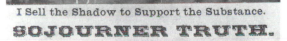

I Sell the Shadow to Support the Substance.

SOJOURNER TRUTH.

Sojourner also spoke at women's **rights** meetings. She said that as a slave, she worked just as hard as men, even though she was a woman. "I have plowed and **reaped** and husked and chopped and mowed, " she said. "I can carry as much as a man, and can eat as much too, if I can get it. I am as strong as any man that is now." She told men to give women their rights.

19

The **Civil War** started in 1861. People in the North thought the U.S. government, or **Union**, should be more powerful than the states. Northerners also wanted to outlaw slavery. People in the South believed states should have more power. They felt they needed slaves to work on their large farms. The war started when the Southern states decided to separate from the Union.

Sojourner spoke at the same meetings as another former slave, Frederick Douglass. He thought it would take **violence** to end slavery. Sojourner hoped he was wrong, but he was right.

The photograph in Sojourner's lap is probably of her grandson, James Caldwell. He fought in an all-black unit during the Civil War.

In 1863, the Union Army decided to allow black soldiers. Sojourner encouraged black men to join. Her grandson, James Caldwell, signed up. He wrote to Sojourner, "Now is our time, Grandmother, to prove that we are men."

By now, Sojourner was living in the area of Battle Creek, Michigan. She brought donations of food to nearby black troops for a Thanksgiving dinner.

Helping Freed Slaves

During and after the war, many freed slaves traveled to Washington, D.C. They didn't have money or jobs, so they lived in camps built by the government. In 1864, Sojourner went to Washington to visit the freed slaves. She stayed for two years, giving out donations of food and clothing. She also helped blacks find jobs and places to live in Northern cities.

These freed slaves are holding an outdoor church service at a camp in Washington, D.C. Sojourner raised money to provide food and clothing for many freed slaves.

In this painting, President Lincoln shows Sojourner a beautiful Bible given to him by a group of black people from Baltimore, Maryland.

While in Washington, Sojourner met with President Abraham Lincoln. She told the president that she respected him for helping to end slavery. President Lincoln signed her **autograph** book with the words, "For Aunty Sojourner Truth." Sojourner later said, "I felt that I was in the presence of a friend."

In 1865, a new law said blacks could ride inside the **streetcars** in Washington, D.C. But many drivers refused to pick up black people. Sojourner forced her way on. Once she yelled, "I WANT TO RIDE!" until the driver stopped. Sojourner reported drivers who gave her trouble to the streetcar company. They lost their jobs. Drivers soon realized they had to follow the law.

In the 1800s, streetcars pulled by horses provided transportation in major cities. In 1865, a new Washington, D.C., law allowed blacks to ride inside streetcars instead of only on the outside platforms.

24

Sojourner is about 73 years old in this photograph. She continued to speak out for the rights of blacks and women throughout her later years.

After the war, freed slaves needed homes and jobs. Sojourner thought the government should give blacks some land in the **West**. She asked people to sign petitions. People who signed these papers said they agreed with this idea. Sojourner sent the petitions to members of the government, but nothing happened. By 1879, many blacks were moving west on their own.

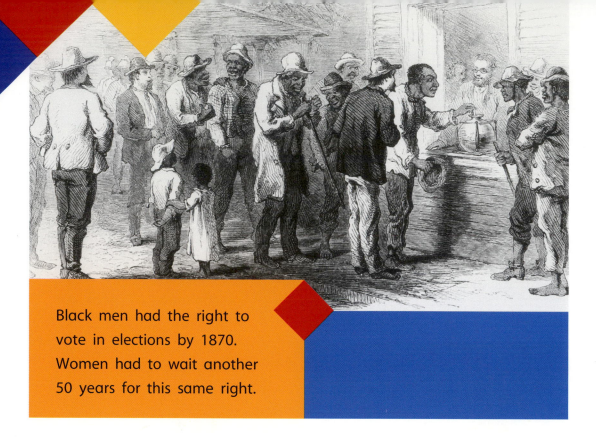

Black men had the right to vote in elections by 1870. Women had to wait another 50 years for this same right.

In 1870, black men received the right to vote. Sojourner wanted all women to have this right, too. She said, "You [men] have been having our right[s] so long, that you think, like a slaveholder, that you own us."

Sojourner tried to vote in the 1872 elections, but officials turned her away. Women did not receive the right to vote until 1920.

In 1883, Sojourner became very ill. She died on November 26 at the age of 86. Though born a slave, Sojourner had the courage to take freedom for herself. She shared her story to bring hope to others. She spoke out against slavery and for women's rights. Today, people still remember Sojourner for helping others.

Sojourner lived in the Battle Creek area for about 26 years of her life. In 1999, an artist created this monument for the city. It shows Sojourner preaching.

Important Dates in Sojourner's Life

1797—Isabella is born near Hurley, New York; her family is owned by the Hardenberghs.

 1808—Isabella is sold to John Neely.

1809—Isabella is sold to Martinus Schryver.

1810—Isabella is sold to John Dumont.

1817—New York passes a law that would give most adult slaves their freedom in 1827.

1826—Isabella leaves the Dumont farm with her baby, Sophia; the Van Wagenens buy them and give them their freedom.

1828—Isabella takes Solomon Gedney to court for selling her son, Peter, out of state; the judge gives Peter to Isabella.

1829—Isabella moves to New York City with Peter.

 1843—Isabella changes her name to Sojourner Truth and begins to travel.

1850—*The Narrative of Sojourner Truth* is published; Sojourner starts speaking at abolition and women's rights meetings; she buys her own house in Northampton, Massachusettes.

1857—Sojourner sells her first house and buys a house in Harmonia, Michigan, near the city of Battle Creek.

1861—The Civil War begins.

1864—Sojourner goes to Washington, D.C., to help freed slaves; she meets President Abraham Lincoln.

1865—The Civil War ends.

1867—Sojourner buys another house in Battle Creek; she travels to Kansas to help freed slaves moving west.

 1883—Sojourner Truth dies at her home in Battle Creek.

1981—Sojourner is selected to be in the National Women's Hall of Fame in Seneca Falls, New York.

More about the Struggle for Rights

In the mid-1800s, the goals of abolitionists and women's rights groups were closely connected. Slaves held no rights in most states, and women held very few.

Owners treated their slaves as property. They beat their slaves and made them work long hours. Often slaves went hungry and didn't have a decent place to live. Laws did not protect slaves. In the early 1800s, abolitionists started to publish newsletters and hold meetings to tell people about these terrible conditions.

Some women joined the abolition movement. They began to see how their own rights were limited. They were expected to mind their husbands and not voice their own opinions. Usually only lower-class women worked outside the home. Only certain jobs were available to them, such as cooking or washing clothes. Women could not vote, and in some cases, they could not inherit property or go to college. Soon women abolitionists began to speak out for women's rights. In 1848, about 300 women and men attended the first Women's Rights Convention, held in Seneca Falls, New York.

Women march for the right to vote. The women's rights movement grew out of the abolition movement in the mid-1800s.

Sojourner Truth spoke for both abolition and women's rights groups. At conventions, she told people not to "beg for their rights," but "to rise up and take them." She had lived out this advice. She freed herself from slavery and later chose to become a traveling preacher.

In 1870, the 15th Amendment passed, giving black men the right to vote. Sojourner and other women's rights activists believed if black men had the right to vote, all women should too. For 50 years, women continued the fight. In 1920, the 19th Amendment finally gave women nationwide the right to vote.

Glossary

abolitionist—a person who works to end, or abolish, slavery

auction—a sale where items are sold to the person with the highest bid, or offer of money

autograph—a person's name, written by the person in his or her own style; Sojourner had a book that she asked people to autograph; she called it her Book of Life.

Civil War—the U.S. war between the Northern and the Southern states that lasted from 1861 to 1865

debate—to discuss both sides of an issue, or to talk about different views

Dutch—people from a small country in Europe called the Netherlands; also, the language spoken by this group of people

ferry—a boat that carries people across a stretch of water

narrative—a story or description of something that happened

Quaker—someone who follows the Quaker religion; Quakers hold simple religious services; they are against slavery and war.

reap—to cut grain or gather a crop when it is ripe

religious—having to do with your religion or belief in God or gods

rights—something that the law says you can have or do; today some basic rights in the United States are the right to own property, the right to equal treatment under the law, and the right to vote.

slave—a person who is owned by another person and thought of as property

streetcar—a type of transportation, usually in a city; in Sojourner's time, streetcars were enclosed wagons pulled by horses.

Union—the United States of America; also, the states that remained loyal to the U.S. government during the Civil War

violence—to use physical force that could cause damage or hurt someone

West—lands in the western part of the United States; in Sojourner's day, the West referred to land west of the Mississippi River; most of this land had yet to be settled.

To Learn More

Read these books:

Adler, David A. *A Picture Book of Sojourner Truth*. New York: Holiday House, 1994.

Frost, Helen. *Sojourner Truth*. Famous Americans. Mankato, Minn.: Pebble Books, 2003.

Jaffe, Elizabeth Dana. *Sojourner Truth*. Compass Point Early Biographies. Minneapolis: Compass Point Books, 2001.

Rockwell, Anne. *Only Passing Through: The Story of Sojourner Truth*. New York: Alfred A. Knopf, 2000.

Look up these Web sites:

American Writers: Sojourner Truth

www.americanwriters.org/archives/player/truth.htm

View video clips of interviews and meetings related to Sojourner Truth. Of special interest are the videos of the Sojourner Truth portrayer, Alice McGill, and the tour of the Sojourner Truth Monument in Battle Creek, Michigan.

National Women's Hall of Fame: Sojourner Truth

www.greatwomen.org/women.php?action=viewone&id=158

Sojourner Truth was named to this Hall of Fame in 1981. Click on "Our History" at the top to learn more about the women's rights movement.

On the Trail of Sojourner Truth

www.newpaltz.edu/sojourner_truth/

Explore this collection of stories, artwork, and photographs related to Sojourner. View photographs of the houses where Sojourner may have lived.

Key Internet search terms:

Sojourner Truth, slavery, abolition, women's rights

Index

a

abolitionists, 18, 27–29

c

Caldwell, James (grandson), 21
Civil War, 20–21, 28

d

Diana (daughter), 7
Douglass, Frederick, 20
Dumont, John, 7–10, 12, 14, 28

e

Elizabeth (mother), 4
Elizabeth (daughter), 7

g

Gedney, Solomon, 10–11, 28
Gilbert, Olive, 18

h

Hardenbergh Family, 5–6, 28

j

James (father), 4

l

Lincoln, Abraham, President, 23, 28

n

Narrative of Sojourner Truth, 18, 28
National Women's Hall of Fame, 28
Neely Family, 6, 28
Northampton Association, 18

p

Peter (brother), 4
Peter (son), 7, 10–14, 28

q

Quakers, 10–11

s

Schryver, Martinus, 6, 28
slavery, 4-10, 18-23, 28-29
Sophia (daughter), 7, 9, 12, 28

t

Truth, Sojourner (Isabella)
  and abolitionists, 18, 27–29
  birth of, 4, 28
  death of, 27–28
  faith of, 6, 14, 17
  lectures of, 14–19, 27–29
  name change of, 15, 28
  The Narrative of Sojourner Truth, 18, 28
  as slave, 4–8, 17, 27–29
  and streetcar laws, 24
  support of black soldiers, 21
  support of freed slaves, 22–25, 27–28
  and women's rights, 19, 25–29

u

Union Army, 21

v

Van Wagenen Family, 9, 28

w

women's rights, 19, 25–29